Henry Hippo

Jenny Dooley – Virginia Evans

Express Publishing

Picture Dictionary

Jenny Dooley – Virginia Evans

Express Publishing

stuck in the mud!

Hippos love to roll in mud,
Roll in mud, roll in mud!
Rocking, rolling – feeling fine
Having such a muddy time!

Down by the river
On a sunny day,
Rocking and rolling,
It is time to play!

Look at Henry Hippo run!
He's having fun out in the sun!

Down to the river, hip, hip, hooray!
It's such a lovely day to play!

Oh, dear, oh dear! This isn't good –
Look at me, I'm stuck in the mud!

Help me, help me! Help me, please!
I'm in the mud up to my knees!

Peter Panda's out today
It's such a lovely day to play!

Down to the river, pitter patter,
Henry Hippo! What's the matter?

Oh, dear, oh dear! This isn't good –
Look at me, I'm stuck in the mud!

Help me, Peter! Help me, please!
I'm in the mud up to my knees!

Okay, Henry! Wish me luck!

He pulls and pulls, but Henry's stuck!

I'm sorry, Henry. Please don't cry,
Here comes Millie! She can try!

Millie Monkey's out today
It's such a lovely day to play!

Down to the river, pitter patter,
Henry Hippo! What's the matter?

Oh, dear, oh dear! This isn't good –
Look at me, I'm stuck in the mud!

Help me, Millie! Help me, please!
I'm in the mud up to my knees!

Okay, Henry! Wish me luck!

She pulls and pulls, but Henry's stuck!

I'm sorry, Henry. Please don't cry,
Here comes Zara! She can try!

Zara Zebra's out today
It's such a lovely day to play!

Down to the river, pitter patter,
Henry Hippo! What's the matter?

Oh, dear, oh dear! This isn't good –
Look at me, I'm stuck in the mud!

Help me, Zara! Help me, please!
I'm in the mud up to my knees!

Okay, Henry! Wish me luck!

She pulls and pulls, but Henry's stuck!

I'm sorry Henry. Please don't cry!
There's one more thing that we can try.

It's no good my friends! I'm stuck forever!

Let's all try to pull him together!

And so the friends get in a group –
They pull and pull – then GLOOP, GLOOP, GLOOP!

Free at last! Hip, hip, hooray!
Thank you, friends. Let's go and play!

Happy now, they understand
That friends work better hand in hand!

Pull together!

Pull, pull, pull together,
Make a happy team.
When your friends all pull together,
Things work like a dream!

Picture Dictionary

ANIMALS

hippo

panda

monkey

zebra

VERBS

roll

play

run

pull

cry

NOUNS

mud

stuck

sun

river

team

knee

dream

Now let's act it out!

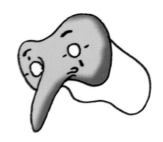

Characters: Narrator
Henry Hippo
Peter Panda
Millie Monkey
Zara Zebra

Narrator: Look at Henry Hippo run!
He's having fun out in the sun!
Down to the river, hip, hip, hooray!
It's such a lovely day to play!

Henry Hippo: Oh, dear, oh dear! This isn't good – Look at me, I'm stuck in the mud!
Help me, help me! Help me, please!
I'm in the mud up to my knees!

Narrator: Peter Panda's out today
It's such a lovely day to play!

Peter Panda: Down to the river, pitter patter,
Henry Hippo! What's the matter?

Henry Hippo:	Oh, dear, oh dear! This isn't good – Look at me, I'm stuck in the mud! Help me, Peter! Help me, please! I'm in the mud up to my knees!
Peter Panda:	Okay, Henry! Wish me luck!
Narrator:	He pulls and pulls, but Henry's stuck!
Peter Panda:	I'm sorry, Henry. Please don't cry, Here comes Millie! She can try!
Narrator:	Millie Monkey's out today It's such a lovely day to play!
Millie Monkey:	Down to the river, pitter patter, Henry Hippo! What's the matter?
Henry Hippo:	Oh, dear, oh dear! This isn't good – Look at me, I'm stuck in the mud! Help me, Millie! Help me, please! I'm in the mud up to my knees!

Millie Monkey:	Okay, Henry! Wish me luck!
Narrator:	She pulls and pulls, but Henry's stuck!
Millie Monkey:	I'm sorry, Henry. Please don't cry,
	Here comes Zara! She can try!
Narrator:	Zara Zebra's out today
	It's such a lovely day to play!
Zara Zebra:	Down to the river, pitter patter,
	Henry Hippo! What's the matter?
Henry Hippo:	Oh, dear, oh dear! This isn't good – Look at me, I'm stuck in the mud!
	Help me, Zara! Help me, please!
	I'm in the mud up to my knees!
Zara Zebra:	Okay, Henry! Wish me luck!
Narrator:	She pulls and pulls, but Henry's stuck!

Zara Zebra:	I'm sorry Henry. Please don't cry! There's one more thing that we can try.
Henry Hippo:	It's no good my friends! I'm stuck forever!
Zara Zebra:	Let's all try to pull him together!
Narrator:	And so the friends get in a group – They pull and pull – then GLOOP, GLOOP, GLOOP!
Henry Hippo:	Free at last! Hip, hip, hooray! Thank you, friends. Let's go and play!
Narrator:	Happy now, they understand That friends work better hand in hand!